A Mother's Goal…

to create a resilient heart

Antonette Taylor

AuthorHouse™
1663 Liberty Drive
Bloomington, IN 47403
www.authorhouse.com
Phone: 833-262-8899

Because of the dynamic nature of the Internet, any web addresses or links contained in this book may have changed since publication and may no longer be valid. The views expressed in this work are solely those of the author and do not necessarily reflect the views of the publisher, and the publisher hereby disclaims any responsibility for them.

Any people depicted in stock imagery provided by Getty Images are models, and such images are being used for illustrative purposes only.
Certain stock imagery © Getty Images.

This book is printed on acid-free paper.

ISBN: 978-1-4389-8600-5 (sc)

Print information available on the last page.

Published by AuthorHouse 07/22/2022

This book is dedicated to my children Lauryn and Brandon. I have been blessed with two of the most incredible children God could have put on earth. I love you both with my entire heart and soul and hope you find this book to be a reminder of what I wish for you.

Introduction

As a parent, you know parenting is the most difficult job you will ever perform. I have become a much better parent as I progress in this role; however, I still make mistakes and need much growth. What I've realized is that we take the good, and the bad, from our upbringing and make the most, and the best, for our children. I don't think parenting can ever be perfected, but it is all about how hard you try and how much you care.

As we all should know, parenting is the most significant role one can ever perform because the outcome is the individual you create. I hope this book inspires all of us to think about what we want for our children on an ongoing basis and convey those thoughts to them consistently.

Because I believe in teaching my children to help those in need, 50% of the profits will be donated to RADkids.org.

TO: Mom
from:
Lauryn!

I believe
in you
Mom so
mush. I ♥ u!

For my children to become individuals who take their pain and do something great with it.

For my children not to accept "I don't know." as an answer from themselves regarding their inner conflicts, thoughts and emotions.

For my children to learn how to give the gifts within themselves.

For my children to know people will forget what you say, they will forget what you do, but they never forget how you make them feel.

For my children to know at the age of 60, you fear not seeing those you love, at 30, you fear the call knowing you didn't say goodbye, and in your teens, you have no fear.

For my children to be conscious that only they have the power to choose who they want to be.

For my children to honor and emulate those who have accomplished significant change: Martin Luther King Jr., Gloria Steinem, Walter Payton, Oprah Winfrey, Nelson Mandela, Princess Diana, Mattie Stepanek, Barack Obama and more.

For my children to encounter opportunity by learning how to open doors for themselves.

For my children to know that fear is a friend that is misunderstood and courage is a friend that is neglected.

For my children not to allow their disappointments to paralyze them.

For my children to build on the foundation they decide.

For my children to visualize their dreams and never allow life's hardships and disappointments to stop them from dreaming.

For my children to know saying too much is better than not saying what you need to say.

For my children to seize control when they become too comfortable.

For my children to approach problems as a friend.

For my children to care about people.

For my children to discover what their passion is and give that to the world.

For my children to be aware that freeing your mind of stress will help you make better choices.

For my children to have lots of dogs like Snow.

For my children to realize, at some point, you have to stop dreaming and start living it.

For my children to think the sound of their children is beautiful.

For my children to possess intellectual depth.

For my children to acknowledge teachers are a gift from God and deserve to be treated with respect and praise.

For my children to _____

For my children to _____

mom THANK YOU FOR SIGNING ME UP FOR FOOTBALL.

XOXO

I ♡U mom

For my children to understand the most important person they have is themselves.

For my children to love with their whole heart & soul.

For my children to have stories to share.

For my children to know they can be a hero by just being there for the ones they love.

For my children to explore the world and learn different cultures.

For my children to understand the value of an individual's life is measured by how deeply he/she has touched the lives of others.

For my children to be strong individuals mentally, physically and emotionally.

For my children to be aware that leaving the past behind is okay.

For my children to respect their parents because they've earned it.

For my children to be appreciative individuals.

For my children to understand the benefits of making sacrifices.

For my children to be great at building relationships of all levels and degrees.

For my children to learn that if you don't quit, you won't give up.

For my children to appreciate the little things in life.

For my children to master empathy and make that part of who they are.

For my children to be effective sales people regardless of the profession they choose.

For my children to obey rules.

For my children to embrace the gift of the presence.

For my children to emulate what they admire about those they respect and love.

For my children to know when you step in to fear, you will be successful.

For my children to learn strength through their weaknesses.

For my children to engage their heart & mind in all that they do.

For my children to see the beauty in all that is.

For my children to acknowledge the difference between a job & a career.

For my children to empower their fears to become their strengths.

For my children to reach out in to the world and make what is meant happen.

For my children to embrace the presence of those they love.

For my children to see my eyes shine when I look at them.

For my children to _____

For my children to _____

To: Mom and Dad
from: Lauryn

For my children to have a soft heart.

For my children to have play dates for their children.

For my children to command respect because they've earned it, and to desire being respected.

For my children to think of themselves as a wish granted.

For my children to be continually conscious of the power of forgiveness.

For my children to identify their passion.

For my children to be okay with receiving.

For my children to persevere through their most challenging times.

For my children to possess the courage to seek what they need to feed their souls.

For my children to teach other people how to become what they want to be.

For my children to embrace aging.

For my children to cultivate wealth and diminish debt.

For my children to know it is okay to express their emotions.

For my children to learn how to communicate in every aspect of their lives.

For my children to learn compassion and become compassionate.

For my children to be happy and fun.

For my children to love and embrace their family and friends.

For my children to help and pray for those in need.

For my children to forgive themselves when they have made a mistake and grow from the experience.

For my children to only marry someone they're in love with.

For my children to love passionately.

For my children to learn the gift of forgiveness.

For my children to dream as big as they can.

For my children to challenge themselves to always be better.

For my children to say thank you and please without a second thought.

For my children to dwell only long enough to learn and then move on.

For my children to give when they think they can't.

For my children to know it is okay to feel what they're feeling.

For my children to say sorry when they need to.

For my children to _____

For my children to _____

For my children to say I love you as much as they can to those they love.

For my children to know negative energy is contagious.

For my children to be independent, but ask for help when they need to.

For my children to be affectionate with their children and the ones they love.

For my children to see the glass ½ full.

For my children not to judge others, but to respect their individuality.

For my children to love unconditionally.

For my children to embrace education and all that it has to offer.

For my children to become financially wealthy.

For my children to learn how to hear the music of their soul.

For my children to know how to express what they're feeling.

For my children to have a conscience.

For my children to confidently know they can tell me anything and I will always love them.

For my children to learn how to fight for what they believe in and not give up.

For my children to practice trusting their inner instincts.

For my children to feel loved more than anything in the world.

For my children to feel safe and wanted.

For my children to embrace life.

For my children to be thoughtful and considerate.

For my children to have courage.

For my children to listen with their heart.

For my children to have a voice in the world.

For my children to have inner beauty.

For my children to be the best person they can be even when they feel life is unfair.

For my children not to judge or criticize until they've walked in the shoes of those they dare to judge or criticize.

For my children to honor themselves.

For my children to know that truly loving another begins with loving themselves.

For my children to learn the power of negotiation.

For my children to _____

For my children to _____

Mom,
I love you with
all my heart.

♥ →

mytkal

Thank you
for staying
home and Taking
care of us
I Love You!!
Lautyn ☺

For my children to learn that marriage is about compromising.

For my children to know that being a parent is the greatest gift God blessed me with.

For my children to learn that hardships are a blessing in disguise.

For my children to be tenacious.

For my children to find a companion who can't bear to see them in pain.

For my children not to believe anyone who tells them they can't.

For my children to know it is okay to tell someone you need them.

For my children to know moods are contagious.

For my children to love exercising not just for their physical being, but for their health.

For my children to become emotionally wealthy by making deposits in their emotional bank account.

For my children to celebrate and learn from the success of others.

For my children to learn from my mistakes.

For my children not to take life for granted.

For my children not to have hatred.

For my children to give back to the world.

For my children to learn the more you give the more it comes back to you.

For my children to know no color when they look into the heart and soul of another.

For my children to conquer fear of getting their heart broken.

For my children to do unto others as they want done to them.

For my children to invest in real estate as they become young adults.

For my children to understand the sacrifices parents make.

For my children to be leaders.

For my children to *always* be truthful to themselves.

For my children to work hard for what they want.

For my children to have endurance.

For my children to hold their children for as long as they can.

For my children to have many true friends.

For my children to respect people's opinions, beliefs and most importantly their individuality.

For my children to _____

For my children to _____

Dear Mom I♡you

From,

Brandon

For my children to know I will always be there for them.

For my children not to allow life's hardships change their inner beauty or who they are.

For my children to set high standards for themselves.

For my children to acknowledge every day they awake is a blessing.

For my children to be happy with their inner and outer being.

For my children to possess character and own who they are.

For my children to touch many lives in a meaningful way.

For my children to conduct themselves professionally in their careers.

For my children to be financially savvy.

For my children to seek understanding, before being understood.

For my children to learn that we need to be each other's coaches.

For my children to strive to be proud of their children.

For my children to realize they always have a choice even when it doesn't seem so.

For my children to love our family.

For my children to feel with their heart and soul.

For my children to practice thinking with logic versus emotion.

For my children to embrace that mommy & daddy love each other.

For my children not to blame others but to look within first.

For my children to learn how to compromise.

For my children to be team players.

For my children to overcome fear with action.

For my children to learn how to run a household.

For my children to give from their hearts without expecting something in return.

For my children to be able to figure out what they feel and then express it to those they need to.

For my children to visualize their dreams until they realize them.

For my children to own a big heart.

For my children to give themselves one of the greatest gifts: to believe in themselves.

For my children to strive to be the most beautiful, tender, wonderful and fantastic beings they can.

For my children to _____

For my children to _____

For my children to deliver constructive criticism with praise as the predecessor.

For my children to achieve the highest level of education they can.

For my children to learn that a winner has fun playing the game.

For my children to understand that attitude determines altitude.

For my children to realize it is okay to lose because sometimes that is how you learn the most.

For my children to realize they are a product of what we've made them to be.

For my children to know their friends are the family they choose.

For my children to be a true friend.

For my children to realize their full potential and be successful.

For my children to provide a happy & healthy home for their children.

For my children to infuse their lives with love.

For my children to inspire others.

For my children to be humble.

For my children to be accountable for their actions and choices.

For my children to be wise investors.

For my children to know when to say goodbye.

For my children to feel deep.

For my children to live their lives so they have no regrets.

For my children to own their mistakes and make a decision to change their future.

For my children to possess pride, determination and resilience.

For my children to realize your heart will determine how far you go.

For my children to find someone who will love them with their whole heart and soul.

For my children to possess a high standard of ethics and morals.

For my children to have a first love, a true love and an endless love.

For my children to want to be themselves.

For my children to choose being conscious rather than unconscious.

For my children to touch many lives in a positive, productive and effective way.

For my children to open hearts that want to help them achieve something greater.

For my children to _____

For my children to _____

For my children to create their own beautiful poetry, art, music or any self expression.

For my children to commend those who deserve to be.

For my children to become more of who they are.

For my children to possess physical strength that surpasses their pain.

For my children to compliment everyone's inner beauty.

For my children to own their weaknesses.

For my children to possess integrity.

For my children to realize they can be *anything* they set their mind and heart to.

For my children to resist fast forwarding their lives.

For my children not to say yes out of fear, but to say no out of love.

For my children to be fearless when expressing their emotions.

For my children to be the best parents they can be.

For my children to choose happiness even at the expense of ending a marriage.

For my children to respect and honor the people they love.

For my children to embrace the power of forgiveness.

For my children to prepare for the future.

For my children to love raising their children.

For my children to teach praise.

For my children to realize communication is the key to success in every aspect of life.

For my children to cherish, and not take for granted, their loved ones.

For my children to realize their thoughts create their life.

For my children to choose and practice acknowledgement.

For my children to conquer their disconnections.

For my children to embrace different cultures.

For my children to listen passionately.

For my children to command equality in all of their relationships.

For my children to be emotionally healthy and successful.

For my children to own dignity.

For my children to be organized.

For my children to strengthen their hearts through disappointments.

For my children to _____

For my children to _____

Dad,
I Love you and
Thank you for
~~pl~~ Playing with
us even if you are
~~my Tony~~

Tiered from
work.
I Love you
with 🖤 all my
heart!! moryn

For my children to acknowledge the heart can only heal when you allow it to feel.

For my children to reveal their vulnerabilities without allowing it to weaken them.

For my children to realize honesty builds character.

For my children to acknowledge that we are equal on a humanity level regardless of what position we're in professionally.

For my children to be relentless in pursuit of their goal.

For my children to know I believe in them.

For my children to become indispensible.

For my children to build character and success through dedication.

For my children to surround themselves by those who choose to build them up not knock them down.

For my children to tackle finances with their spouse as a partnership.

For my children to own a summer home and create memories.

For my children to be proud of their home.